MODERATE LEVEL

MATCHING CHINESE CHARACTERS AND PINYIN

把汉字和拼音连起来

MANDARIN CHINESE PINYIN TEST SERIES

测试你的拼音知识

PART 20

Simplified Mandarin Chinese Characters with Pinyin and English, Mind Games, Test Your Knowledge of Pinyin with Multiple Answer Choice Puzzle Questions, Fast Reading & Vocabulary, Answers Included, Easy Lessons for Beginners, HSK All Levels

DENG YIXIN 邓艺心

ACKNOWLEDGEMENT

I would like to thank everyone who helped me complete this book, including my teachers, family members, friends, colleagues.

谢谢

Deng Yixin

邓艺心

INTRODUCTION

Chinese language and culture are a huge concept. In order to understand and appreciate Mandarin Chinese, we need to understand the language. Learning Chinese character is a very important part of learning the language. And, yes, learning pinyin is a must!

Welcome to **Connecting Chinese Characters and Pinyin Test Series**. Now you can test the knowledge of your Chinese pinyin (测试你的拼音知识). In these books and lessons therein, you will learn recognizing pinyin of the simplified Chinese characters. The books contain hundreds of character-pinyin matching **puzzles** (questions). For each question, there are Chinese characters in the left column and pinyin in the right column. You need to guess the correct pinyin of the given characters (把汉字和拼音连起来). The **English** meanings of the Chinese characters has been included a quick reference. The answers of all the question are provided at the end of the book.

CONTENTS

CHAPTER 1: QUESTIONS (1-30)

#1.

A. 焱   1. Fèi (Fee)

B. 串   2. Biāo (Dashing)

C. 费   3. Chī (Demons)

D. 魑   4. Chuàn (String together)

E. 聸   5. Dān (A word used in a person's name)

#2.

A. 历   1. Lì (Experience)

B. 霈   2. Nì (Hide)

C. 税   3. Shuì (Tax)

D. 匿   4. Pèi (Heavy rain)

E. 坚   5. Jiān (Hard)

#3.

A. 朱   1. Nǐng (Differ)

B. 雀   2. Zhū (Bright red)

C. 拧   3. Qiǎo (Sparrow)

D. 嚏   4. Tì (Sneeze)

E. 嚏   5. Dié (Small melon)

#4.

A. 老   1. Lǎo (Aged)

B. 教   2. Sì (Raise)

C. 厉   3. Lì (Stern)

D. 饲   4. Jiào (Religion)

E. 酷   5. Kù (Cruel)

#5.

A. 冲   1. Piāo (Rob)

B. 敏   2. Mǐn (Quick)

C. 浑   3. Hún (Muddy)

D. 剽   4. Chōng (Thoroughfare)

E. 鹭   5. Lù (Egret)

#6.

A. 式   1. Bó (Rich)

B. 博   2. Shì (Type)

C. 烧   3. Shāo (Burn)

D. 髂   4. Dí (See)

E. 觑
5. Qià (Ilium)

#7.

A. 它
1. Tā (It)

B. 即
2. Jiàng (Paste)

C. 酱
3. Jí (Which is)

D. 量
4. Liáng (Measure)

E. 挖
5. Wā (Dig)

#8.

A. 外
1. Wèi (Wei, a state in the Zhou Dynasty)

B. 卫
2. Tǎn (Leave uncovered)

C. 袒
3. Wài (Outside)

D. 售
4. Shà (A tall building)

E. 厦
5. Shòu (Sell)

#9.

A. 斐
1. Qiè (A surname)

B. 颁
2. Fěi (Rich with literary grace)

C. 飑
3. Ān (Saddle)

D. 郄
4. Bān (Issue)

E. 鞍

5. Zhǎn (Set in motion)

#10.

A. 况

1. Gē (Song)

B. 歌

2. Kuàng (Condition)

C. 汍

3. Yào (Sunlight)

D. 曜

4. Wán (Weeping)

E. 猪

5. Zhū (Hog)

#11.

A. 医

1. Sōu (Make sth. dry or cool)

B. 驿

2. Bà (Dam)

C. 坝

3. Yì (Station)

D. 飕

4. Yī (Doctor)

E. 恙

5. Yàng (Ailment)

#12.

A. 矽

1. Tuì (Scald in order to remove hairs or feathers)

B. 递

2. Wēng (Old man)

C. 倾

3. Qīng (Incline)

D. 煺

4. Dì (Handover)

E. 翁   5. Kū (Toil)

#13.

A. 醍   1. Tí (Red wine)

B. 清   2. Luó (Patrol)

C. 钱   3. Qián (Copper coin)

D. 逻   4. Lǐn (Cold)

E. 凛   5. Qìng (Chilly)

#14.

A. 灼   1. Liè (Arrange)

B. 喆   2. Zhé (A wise and intelligent person)

C. 轼   3. Shì (A horizontal bar in front of a carriage for armrest)

D. 江   4. Zhuó (Burn)

E. 列   5. Gāng (A surname)

#15.

A. 齐   1. Qí (Neat)

B. 蛾   2. Pǐ (Be equal to)

C. 匹   3. Cān (Eat)

D. 餐   4. Pī (Young raccoon)

E. 豵   5. É (Moth)

#16.

A. 绥   1. Suí (Peaceful)

B. 霆   2. Tāng (Loosen the soil and dig up weeds with a rake or
a hoe)

C. 买   3. Tíng (Thunder)

D. 应   4. Mǎi (Buy)

E. 耥   5. Yīng (Should)

#17.

A. 魂   1. Kuí (Path)

B. 炎   2. Chì (Imperial order)

C. 环   3. Huán (Ring)

D. 敕   4. Yán (Scorching)

E. 馗   5. Hún (Soul)

#18.

A. 飒   1. Jiē (All)

B. 尽   2. Fēng (Sound of the flowing water)

C. 皆   3. Yǔ (Disagreement (the upper and lower teeth not
meeting properly))

D. 猴   4. Hóu (Monkey)

E. 龉   5. Jǐn (To the greatest extent)

#19.

A. 褪   1. Pàn (Betray)

B. 叛   2. Qiān (Thousand)

C. 索   3. Tùn (Slip out of sth)

D. 詈   4. Suǒ (Cable)

E. 千   5. Lì (Scold)

#20.

A. 轨   1. Liú (Flow)

B. 流   2. Sān (Three)

C. 怪   3. Guǐ (Rail)

D. 叁   4. Fú (Tally)

E. 符   5. Guài (Strange)

#21.

A. 贞   1. Lào (Level)

B. 丁   2. Dīng (Surname)

C. 耢   3. Zhēn (Loyal)

D. 鸳

4. Yāng (Mandarin duck)

E. 鹘

5. Hú (Falcon)

#22.

A. 驭

1. Bì (Give)

B. 畀

2. Duàn (Break)

C. 骸

3. Diān (Mentally deranged)

D. 癫

4. Yù (Control)

E. 断

5. Hái (Body)

#23.

A. 郜

1. Zhēn (Genuine)

B. 识

2. Zhì (Remember)

C. 真

3. Gào (A surname)

D. 鳏

4. Wù (In tranquil)

E. 阢

5. Guān (Huge fish)

#24.

A. 窗

1. Kuí (A one-legged monster in the fables)

B. 夔

2. Chuāng (Window)

C. 鸭

3. Xīng (Prosper)

D. 兴

E. 规

4. Guī (Rule)

5. Yā (Duck)

#25.

A. 艒

B. 泼

C. 醝

D. 衲

E. 弱

1. Nà (Patch up)

2. Ruò (Weak)

3. Mù (Boat)

4. Pō (Sprinkle)

5. Cuō (White spirit)

#26.

A. 陫

B. 舰

C. 弃

D. 笑

E. 泫

1. Xiào (Smile)

2. Xuàn (Drip)

3. Qì (Throw away)

4. Péi (Wall)

5. Jiàn (Warship)

#27.

A. 冬

B. 谦

C. 皋

1. Dōng (Winter)

2. Gāo (Marshland)

3. Sì (A team of four horses)

D. 竟   4. Qiān (Modest)

E. 驷   5. Jìng (Finish)

#28.

A. 耖   1. Chào (A harrow-like implement for pulverizing soil)

B. 胖   2. Zǎo (Flea)

C. 斧   3. Dàn (Egg)

D. 蛋   4. Pàng (Fat)

E. 蚤   5. Fǔ (Axe)

#29.

A. 丰   1. Páng (Other)

B. 旁   2. Mán (Steamed bread)

C. 赤   3. Chì (Red)

D. 忞   4. Fēng (Abundance)

E. 馒   5. Mín (Exert oneself)

#30.

A. 答   1. Liàng (Measure)

B. 虐   2. Nüè (Cruel)

C. 量   3. Bì (Gushed spring water)

D. 轰   4. Dá (Answer)

E. 泌   5. Hōng (Bang)

CHAPTER 2: QUESTIONS (31-60)

#31.

A. 再   1. Zhōu (Congee)

B. 袆   2. Huī (A pheasant pattern on the clothes)

C. 禁   3. Jīn (Bear)

D. 同   4. Zài (Again)

E. 粥   5. Tóng (Same)

#32.

A. 卜   1. Yuān (Kite)

B. 畈   2. Bǔ (Divination)

C. 鸢   3. Fàn (Farmland, often used in place names)

D. 联   4. Zhǐ (Small islets)

E. 沚   5. Lián (Unite)

#33.

A. 主   1. Qiǎo (Skillful)

B. 缙   2. Jìn (Red silk)

C. 巧   3. Mì (Secrete)

D. 悟   4. Zhǔ (Host)

E. 泌 5. Wù (Understand)

#34.

A. 邻 1. Shāo (Whiplash)

B. 鞑 2. Dá (Tatars)

C. 焦 3. Lín (Neighbor)

D. 转 4. Zhuǎn (Change)

E. 鞘 5. Jiāo (Burnt)

#35.

A. 独 1. Láng (An ancient official title)

B. 珀 2. Zhǐ (An ancient measure of length, equal to 8 cun)

C. 豪 3. Dú (Single)

D. 郎 4. Háo (A person of extraordinary powers or endowments)

E. 咫 5. Pò (Amber)

#36.

A. 脸 1. Qiǎo (Skillful)

B. 尧 2. Liǎn (Face)

C. 唐 3. Zhǐ (Small islets)

D. 巧 4. Táng (For nothing)

E. 沝   5. Yáo (Yao, a legendary monarch in ancient China)

#37.

A. 翔   1. Shāng (Wine cup)

B. 觞   2. Zhǔ (Host)

C. 凼   3. Dàng (Water puddle)

D. 主   4. Hǎo (Good)

E. 好   5. Xiáng (Circle in the air)

#38.

A. 观   1. Dèng (Deng, a state in the Zhou Dynasty)

B. 畠   2. Xiòng (A surname)

C. 孵   3. Guān (Observe)

D. 夐   4. Fū (Brood)

E. 邓   5. Tián (Dryland)

#39.

A. 私   1. Lián (Inexpensive)

B. 夜   2. Xiāo (Clouds)

C. 霄   3. Yè (Night)

D. 鹕   4. Sī (Personal)

E. 廉   5. Hú (Swan)

#40.

A. 父   1. Shā (Sand)

B. 瓯   2. Yǒu (Black)

C. 馔   3. Ōu (Bowl)

D. 沙   4. Fù (Father)

E. 黝   5. Zhuàn (Food)

#41.

A. 俄   1. Kān (May)

B. 脚   2. É (Very soon)

C. 堪   3. Jué (Role)

D. 醁   4. Lù (Good wine)

E. 然   5. Rán (Right)

#42.

A. 觫   1. Zhé (Hibernate)

B. 璪   2. Sù (Shiver or tremble from fear)

C. 蛰   3. Zǎo (Silk tassels threaded with jades hanging from a
coronet)

D. 会   4. Kuài (Compute)

E. 瓩   5. Qiān (Kilowatt)

#43.

A. 要   1. Dí (Enemy)

B. 敌   2. Qiān (Modest)

C. 谦   3. Lín (Be close to)

D. 临   4. Bà (Pa)

E. 爸   5. Yāo (Demand)

#44.

A. 卮   1. Lì (A surname)

B. 犯   2. Zhī (An ancient wine vessel)

C. 郦   3. Fàn (Go against)

D. 考   4. Kǎo (Test)

E. 赋   5. Fù (Endow)

#45.

A. 黠   1. Zōng (Ancestor)

B. 胖   2. Cuān (Quick-boil)

C. 宗   3. Pàng (Fat)

D. 汆   4. Huá (Slip)

E. 滑   5. Xiá (Crafty)

#46.

A. 郸   1. Lún (Wheel)

B. 艮   2. Yù (Desire)

C. 部   3. Dān (A surname)

D. 轮   4. Bù (Department)

E. 欲   5. Gěn (Blunt)

#47.

A. 粕   1. Pò (Dregs of rice)

B. 鸣   2. Míng (Cry)

C. 教   3. Liè (Cold)

D. 蹿   4. Jiào (Religion)

E. 冽   5. Cuān (Leap up)

#48.

A. 扁   1. Cù (Kick)

B. 悸   2. Lín (Clear)

C. 光   3. Jì (Throb with terror)

D. 蹴   4. Biǎn (Flat)

E. 粼   5. Guāng (Light)

#49.

A. 膏   1. Qiān (Lead)

B. 鲑   2. Xiè (The legendary god sheep)

C. 盟   3. Míng (Swear)

D. 喆   4. Gāo (Fat)

E. 牵   5. Zhé (A wise and intelligent person)

#50.

A. 沏   1. Qī (Infuse)

B. 豨   2. Xī (Pig)

C. 渣   3. Chào (A harrow-like implement for pulverizing soil)

D. 耖   4. Liáng (Cold)

E. 凉   5. Zhā (Dregs)

#51.

A. 浇   1. Xū (Need)

B. 需   2. Ào (A surname)

C. 项   3. Hū (Neglect)

D. 皴   4. Xiàng (Nape)

E. 忽   5. Cūn (Chapped)

#52.

A. 会   1. Lù (Land)

B. 终   2. Zhōng (End)

C. 陆   3. Nú (Offspring)

D. 孥   4. Sù (Early in the morning)

E. 夙   5. Huì (Get together)

#53.

A. 坛   1. Jié (Section)

B. 节   2. Kě (Bear the load)

C. 坷   3. Náo (A kind of gibbon)

D. 般   4. Bān (Sort)

E. 夒   5. Tán (Altar)

#54.

A. 悄   1. Chèn (Take advantage of)

B. 启   2. Jù (Storm)

C. 厝   3. Qiāo (Quiet)

D. 趁   4. Cuò (Lay)

E. 飓   5. Qǐ (Open)

#55.

A. 卝   1. Kuàng (Hair style)

B. 熏   2. È (Evil)

C. 恶   3. Gòu (Meet)

D. 爱   4. Xūn (Smoke)

E. 覯   5. Ài (Love)

#56.

A. 礼   1. Lǐ (Courtesy)

B. 缀   2. Mì (Secrete)

C. 泌   3. Zhāo (Early morning)

D. 朝   4. Zhuì (Sew)

E. 永   5. Yǒng (Perpetually)

#57.

A. 阮   1. Chūn (Spring)

B. 炼   2. Pì (Brick)

C. 髂   3. Liàn (Refine)

D. 春   4. Qià (Ilium)

E. 罋   5. Ruǎn (Nephew)

#58.

A. 沾   1. Zé (Boat)

B. 是   2. Shì (Yes)

C. 舴   3. Zhān (Wet)

D. 弼   4. Bì (Assist)

E. 凝   5. Níng (Congeal)

#59.

A. 泷   1. Lóng (Rapids)

B. 鹃   2. Róng (Grow luxuriantly)

C. 荣   3. Sòng (Song, a state in the Zhou Dynasty)

D. 宋   4. Juān (Cuckoo)

E. 耪   5. Pǎng (Loosen soil with a hoe)

#60.

A. 町   1. Suí (Peaceful)

B. 腚   2. Biàn (Distinguish)

C. 绥   3. Dìng (Buttocks)

D. 春   4. Tīng (A word used in a place name)

E. 辨

5. Chūn (Spring)

CHAPTER 3: QUESTIONS (61-90)

#61.

A. 坛   1. Tán (Altar)

B. 艋   2. Qiǎn (Shallow)

C. 角   3. Měng (Boat)

D. 关   4. Jué (Role)

E. 浅   5. Guān (Turn off)

#62.

A. 拌   1. Xiàn (Offer)

B. 陋   2. Suàn (Garlic)

C. 前   3. Lòu (Plain)

D. 蒜   4. Bàn (Mix)

E. 献   5. Qián (Front)

#63.

A. 髀   1. Ǎi (Haze)

B. 炸   2. Zhà (Explode)

C. 般   3. Zhǔ (Join)

D. 属   4. Pán (Happy)

E. 靐   5. Bì (Thigh)

#64.

A. 骶   1. Dǐ (Sacrum)

B. 曶   2. Huī (Tease)

C. 诙   3. Guǐ (Sundial)

D. 豪   4. Háo (A person of extraordinary powers or
endowments)

E. 坏   5. Huài (Bad)

#65.

A. 隶   1. Lì (Be subordinate to)

B. 陟   2. Tū (Convex)

C. 脖   3. Zhào (Cover)

D. 凸   4. Bó (Neck)

E. 罩   5. Zhì (Climb)

#66.

A. 串   1. Yàn (Water's edge)

B. 帘   2. Chuàn (String together)

C. 搁   3. Lián (Flag on pole over wine house)

D. 曌   4. Zhào (The name Wu Zetian)

E. 沿   5. Gē (Put)

#67.

A. 坦   1. Tǎn (Level)

B. 媚   2. Mèi (Flatter)

C. 廓   3. Kuò (Outline)

D. 鸭   4. Yā (Duck)

E. 缤   5. Bīn (Abundant)

#68.

A. 拧   1. Guì (Cassia)

B. 欲   2. Yù (Desire)

C. 桂   3. Xiàng (Nape)

D. 浏   4. Liú (Clear)

E. 项   5. Nǐng (Differ)

#69.

A. 欸   1. Zhài (Zhai, a state in the Zhou Dynasty)

B. 胃   2. Gān (Citrus reticulata)

C. 柑   3. Ēi (Hey)

D. 廲   4. Juàn (Hang （挂）)

E. 祭　　　　　　　　5. Yǎn (Black mole)

#70.

A. 皇　　　　　　　　1. Fěi (Cockroach)

B. 隆　　　　　　　　2. Kěn (Earnest)

C. 恳　　　　　　　　3. Qíng (Feeling)

D. 情　　　　　　　　4. Huáng (Grand)

E. 蜚　　　　　　　　5. Lóng (Grand)

#71.

A. 牧　　　　　　　　1. Hàn (Brave)

B. 繁　　　　　　　　2. Nòng (Do)

C. 悍　　　　　　　　3. Pǐ (Be equal to)

D. 弄　　　　　　　　4. Mù (Herd)

E. 匹　　　　　　　　5. Fán (In great number)

#72.

A. 倒　　　　　　　　1. Tí (Pelican)

B. 鹈　　　　　　　　2. Dǎo (Fall)

C. 支　　　　　　　　3. Zhī (Support)

D. 乩　　　　　　　　4. Jiān (Pointed)

E. 尖   5. Shǐ (The beginning)

#73.

A. 艰   1. Jiān (Difficult)

B. 甲   2. Mǎi (Buy)

C. 班   3. Jiǎ (The first of the ten Heavenly Stems)

D. 买   4. Bā (Scar)

E. 疤   5. Bān (Class)

#74.

A. 脸   1. Lǚ (Repeatedly)

B. 戴   2. Qù (Look)

C. 屡   3. Zhàng (Husband)

D. 觑   4. Liǎn (Face)

E. 丈   5. Dài (Put on)

#75.

A. 敖   1. Lín (Neighbor)

B. 邻   2. Xīng (Orangutan)

C. 猩   3. Pà (Fear)

D. 欺   4. Qī (Deceive)

E. 怕   5. Áo (Stroll)

#76.

A. 趟   1. Tàng (Time)

B. 耸   2. Tiǎo (Stir up)

C. 蜀   3. Shǔ (Shu, a state in the Zhou Dynasty)

D. 挑   4. Hóng (Swan goose)

E. 鸿   5. Sǒng (Tower aloft)

#77.

A. 局   1. Quán (Aldehyde)

B. 髈   2. Què (Sparrow)

C. 觅   3. Pǎng (Thigh)

D. 雀   4. Jú (Chessboard)

E. 醛   5. Mì (Look for)

#78.

A. 炭   1. Tú (Slaughter or butcher)

B. 朝   2. Shāng (Wine cup)

C. 屠   3. Zhuàng (Form)

D. 觞   4. Zhāo (Early morning)

E. 状   5. Tàn (Charcoal)

#79.

A. 了   1. Lǜ (Consider)

B. 凿   2. Zuò (Certain)

C. 淑   3. Liào (To survey)

D. 渗   4. Shū (Kind and gentle)

E. 虑   5. Lì (Stagnant)

#80.

A. 覆   1. Yáo (Yao, a legendary monarch in ancient China)

B. 甙   2. Fù (Cover)

C. 黜   3. Chù (Remove sb. from office)

D. 裳   4. Cháng (Skirt (worn in ancient China))

E. 尧   5. Dài (Glucoside)

#81.

A. 救   1. Niàn (Read aloud)

B. 念   2. Jiù (Rescue)

C. 狈   3. Bèi (A wolf-like animal with short forelegs)

D. 类   4. Lèi (Class)

E. 备   5. Bèi (Have)

#82.

A. 韦   1. Wéi (Leather)

B. 千   2. Yì (Adept)

C. 球   3. Qiú (Sphere)

D. 奕   4. Tuì (Scald in order to remove hairs or feathers)

E. 煺   5. Qiān (Thousand)

#83.

A. 耐   1. Nài (Be able to bear or endure)

B. 重   2. Dì (Younger brother)

C. 弟   3. Jú (Tangerine)

D. 苏   4. Chóng (Repeat)

E. 橘   5. Sū (Revive)

#84.

A. 席   1. Yuàn (Courtyard)

B. 院   2. Xí (Seat)

C. 随   3. Suí (Follow)

D. 韦   4. Nóng (Farming)

E. 农   5. Wéi (Leather)

#85.

A. 乐   1. Jì (Reach (a point or a period of time))

B. 罨   2. Yǎn (Net for catching birds or fish)

C. 曾   3. Lè (Happy)

D. 瓠   4. Zēng (Great-grand)

E. 洎   5. Hù (A kind of edible gourd)

#86.

A. 膀   1. Bàng (Row)

B. 醇   2. Shān (Samarium (Sm))

C. 钐   3. Ruǎn (Soft)

D. 软   4. Jiǎo (Horn)

E. 角   5. Bó (Strong aroma)

#87.

A. 馍   1. Fén (The name of a river in Shanxi Province)

B. 汞   2. Bāng (State)

C. 邦   3. Mó (Steamed bread)

D. 汾   4. Rùn (Lubricate)

E. 润   5. Gǒng (Mercury)

#88.

A. 巡   1. Nüè (Malaria)

B. 醴   2. Chǐ (A note of the scale in gongchepu , corresponding
to 2 in numbered musical notation)

C. 疟   3. Yǐ (The appearance of the flags fluttering in the wind)

D. 尺   4. Xún (Patrol)

E. 旖   5. Lǐ (Sweet wine)

#89.

A. 瓢   1. Piáo (Gourd ladle)

B. 粽   2. Zòng (Rice dumplings)

C. 辩   3. Xiàng (Elephant)

D. 象   4. Lèng (Heap)

E. 凌   5. Biàn (Argue)

#90.

A. 痘   1. Wèi (Rising)

B. 价   2. Dòu (Smallpox)

C. 霨   3. Nǎo (Brain)

D. 脑   4. Kuǎn (Sincere)

E. 款   5. Jià (Price)

#91.

A. 包   1. Yuán (Shafts of a cart or carriage)

B. 扈   2. Bāo (Wrap)

C. 辕   3. Jué (Role)

D. 黯   4. Hù (Retainers)

E. 角   5. Àn (Dim)

#92.

A. 伦   1. Chóu (Hatred)

B. 窭   2. Shuì (Tax)

C. 欸   3. Éi (Sigh)

D. 税   4. Jù (Poor)

E. 仇   5. Lún (Order)

#93.

A. 冯   1. Féng (A surname)

B. 殁   2. Gǎn (Dare)

C. 贡   3. Tiǎo (Stir up)

D. 挑   4. Gòng (Pay tribute)

E. 敢   5. Mò (Die)

#94.

A. 购   1. Hú (Complete a set in mahjong)

B. 散   2. Săn (Come loose)

C. 曌   3. Zhào (The name Wu Zetian)

D. 郊   4. Gòu (Purchase)

E. 和   5. Jiāo (Suburbs)

#95.

A. 斑   1. Miù (Pretend)

B. 递   2. Jiào (Check)

C. 缪   3. Dì (Handover)

D. 恶   4. Bān (Spot)

E. 校   5. È (Evil)

#96.

A. 活   1. Yǐ (Ant)

B. 量   2. Zōng (Ancestor)

C. 骱   3. Huó (Live)

D. 蚁   4. Liáng (Measure)

E. 宗   5. Jiè (Joint of bones)

#97.

A. 瓯   1. Xuě (Snow)

B. 臀   2. Qǐng (Qing, a unit of area)

C. 顷   3. Ōu (Bowl)

D. 了   4. Tún (Buttocks)

E. 雪   5. Le (Particle of completed action)

#98.

A. 龉   1. Xī (Pig)

B. 洱   2. Ěr (Er He River (in Henan Province))

C. 弁   3. Qǐ (Open)

D. 启   4. Yǔ (Disagreement (the upper and lower teeth not
meeting properly))

E. 豨   5. Biàn (A man's cap used in ancient times)

#99.

A. 郎   1. Láng (An ancient official title)

B. 医   2. Yī (Doctor)

C. 款   3. Zhì (Place)

D. 置   4. Jù (Distance)

E. 距   5. Kuǎn (Sincere)

#100.

A. 觫   1. Yūn (Agreeable, pleasant)

B. 雏   2. Quǎn (A field ditch)

C. 嫁   3. Jià ((of a woman) to marry a man (opp 娶, qǔ))

D. 赟   4. Sù (Shiver or tremble from fear)

E. 畎   5. Chú (Young)

#101.

A. 俏   1. Fāng (A word used in a place name)

B. 邡   2. Yì (Assist (a ruler))

C. 翊   3. Yíng (Be full of)

D. 盈   4. Qiào (Pretty)

E. 娥   5. É (Pretty young woman)

#102.

A. 耻   1. Cōng (Faculty of hearing)

B. 驽   2. Chǐ (Be ashamed of)

C. 旷   3. Nú (Inferior horse)

D. 聪   4. Kuàng (Vast)

E. 奠

5. Diàn (Establish)

#103.

A. 伐

1. Xiǎng (Feast)

B. 废

2. Gá (Gadolinium (Gd))

C. 袺

3. Jié (Carry sth. in the front of one's jacket)

D. 钆

4. Fèi (Give up)

E. 飨

5. Fá (Fell)

#104.

A. 挛

1. Chào (A harrow-like implement for pulverizing soil)

B. 民

2. Zōu (Zou, a state in the Zhou Dynasty)

C. 篾

3. Mín (The people)

D. 耖

4. Luán (Contraction)

E. 邹

5. Miè (Thin bamboo strip)

#105.

A. 耿

1. Gěng (Shining)

B. 螨

2. Tí (Pelican)

C. 弘

3. Mǎn (Mite)

D. 房

4. Fáng (House)

E. 鹈   5. Hóng (Great)

#106.

A. 嫛   1. Gěn (Blunt)

B. 尔   2. Dān (Single)

C. 单   3. Méi (Broomcorn millet)

D. 縻   4. Ěr (You)

E. 艮   5. Náo (A kind of gibbon)

#107.

A. 月   1. Gǒng (Mercury)

B. 豢   2. Jué (Discontented)

C. 毕   3. Yuè (Moon)

D. 汞   4. Huàn (Feed)

E. 觖   5. Bì (Finish)

#108.

A. 匍   1. Fú (Creep)

B. 盲   2. Shǎo (Few)

C. 欺   3. Qī (Deceive)

D. 飙   4. Biāo (Storm)

E. 少   5. Máng (Blind)

#110.

A. 良   1. Yào (Shine)

B. 耀   2. Jié (Handsome)

C. 背   3. Liáng (Good people)

D. 婕   4. Páo (Roe deer)

E. 狍   5. Bèi (Body's back)

#110.

A. 似   1. Jǐng (Surname)

B. 晕   2. Jù (Straw sandals)

C. 屦   3. Yùn (Halo)

D. 井   4. Xuàn (Jade)

E. 琄   5. Shì (Be similar)

#111.

A. 不   1. Yì (Station)

B. 驿   2. Fèn (Droppings)

C. 冷   3. Bù (Do not)

D. 粪   4. Diāo (Marten)

E. 貂   5. Lěng (Cold)

#112.

A. 蜘   1. Zú (Race)

B. 他   2. Zhī (Spider)

C. 茹   3. Rú (Eat)

D. 族   4. Yán (Scorching)

E. 炎   5. Tā (He)

#113.

A. 皈   1. Guī (Be converted to Buddhism)

B. 对   2. Xiàng (Looks)

C. 相   3. Páo (Prepare Chinese medicine by roasting it in a pan)

D. 炮   4. Shǒu (Stem)

E. 艄   5. Duì (Answer)

#114.

A. 拍   1. Yù (Bring up)

B. 忘   2. Wàng (Forget)

C. 粥   3. Pāi (Shoot)

D. 拿   4. Shā (Personal and place names)

E. 莎   5. Ná (Hold)

#115.

A. 供   1. Ruò (Ruo (the capital of the Chu State))

B. 郶   2. Bèi (A surname)

C. 沛   3. Gōng (Supply)

D. 驯   4. Zuò (Certain)

E. 凿   5. Xún (Tame)

#116.

A. 籴   1. Wán (Pill)

B. 辽   2. Tǔn (Float)

C. 琚   3. Liáo (Distant)

D. 胜   4. Shèng (Win)

E. 丸   5. Jū (Jade pendant)

#117.

A. 盈   1. Shǔ (A government office)

B. 瘰   2. Lù (Egret)

C. 署   3. Fáng (House)

D. 鹭   4. Yíng (Be full of)

E. 房   5. Biě (Shriveled)

#118.

A. 舰   1. Yú (Public)

B. 輿   2. Dǎ (Hit)

C. 刖   3. Jiàn (Warship)

D. 饺   4. Fèi (Amputating the feet)

E. 打   5. Jiǎo (Dumpling)

#119.

A. 浃   1. Lóng (Rapids)

B. 敏   2. Jiā (Soak)

C. 酶   3. Táo (Drunken)

D. 雉   4. Mǐn (Quick)

E. 泷   5. Zhì (Pheasant)

#120.

A. 耧   1. Zhì (Young)

B. 庌   2. Wū (A surname)

C. 醍   3. Tí (Red wine)

D. 稚   4. Lóu (An animal-drawn seed plough)

E. 邬   5. Hù (Bail)

#121.

A. 穌   1. Pēng (Noise of waters)

B. 畏   2. Zōu (Corner)

C. 甸   3. Táng (Birch leaf pear)

D. 棠   4. Wèi (Fear)

E. 陬   5. Sū (Revive)

#122.

A. 豨   1. Xī (Pig)

B. 决   2. Guǎn (Accommodation for guests)

C. 陂   3. Jué (Decide)

D. 馆   4. Páo (Dig ground with foot or hoof)

E. 跑   5. Bēi (Pond)

#123.

A. 糙   1. Wū (What)

B. 於   2. Bāo (Skin)

C. 刺   3. Hésè (Rough)

D. 剥   4. Jiǔ (Collective term for the tribes of northern China during the Liao, Jin, and Yuan periods)

E. 纰   5. Cī (Whoosh (onomatopoeia))

#124.

A. 倾   1. Mò (A kind of beast in ancient books)

B. 貊   2. Qīng (Incline)

C. 医   3. Bǔ (Divination)

D. 卓   4. Yī (Doctor)

E. 卜   5. Zhuō (Table)

#125.

A. 馗   1. Chǎo (Stir-fry)

B. 将   2. Jì (Lonely)

C. 寂   3. Jiàng (General)

D. 馅   4. Kuí (Path)

E. 炒   5. Xiàn (Filling)

#126.

A. 尼   1. Dāng (Work as)

B. 当   2. Ní (Buddhist nun)

C. 启   3. Qǐ (Open)

D. 剐   4. Guǎ (Cut into pieces)

E. 设   5. Shè (Set up)

#127.

A. 鹰   1. Lóu (An animal-drawn seed plough)

B. 耧   2. Yīng (Eagle)

C. 旬   3. Shà (A very short time)

D. 可   4. Xún (A period of ten days)

E. 霎   5. Kě (Approve)

#128.

A. 粒   1. Lì (Small particles)

B. 霡   2. Shā (Personal and place names)

C. 艮   3. gèn (One of the eight trigrams which represents the mountain)

D. 卉   4. Mài (A light rain)

E. 莎   5. Huì ((various kinds of) grass)

#129.

A. 鼓   1. Mián (Cotton)

B. 绿   2. Lǜ (Green)

C. 棉   3. Qiū (A surname)

D. 邱   4. Gǔ (Drum)

E. 范   5. Fàn (Pattern)

#130.

A. 罗   1. Jīn (Muscle)

B. 郡   2. Biāo (Storm)

C. 秋   3. Luō (A net for catching birds)

D. 筋   4. Jùn (Prefecture)

E. 飙   5. Qiū (Autumn)

#131.

A. 粘   1. Jǔ (Stop)

B. 就   2. Shèn (Clams)

C. 沮   3. Jiù (Even if)

D. 罟   4. Yù (Dragnet)

E. 蜃   5. Zhān (Glue)

#132.

A. 袄   1. Yù (Desire)

B. 谊   2. Yì (Friendship)

C. 驴   3. Jiàng (Paste)

D. 欲   4. Ǎo (A short Chinese-style coat or jacket)

E. 酱   5. Lǘ (Donkey)

#133.

A. 旆   1. Zhào (Originate)

B. 孽   2. Zhǐ (Axletree terminal)

C. 轵   3. Huī (Clamor)

D. 肇   4. Pèi (Flag)

E. 厴   5. Niè (Evil)

#134.

A. 宁   1. Níng (Peaceful)

B. 虬   2. Qū (Black)

C. 黢   3. Nòng (Do)

D. 弄   4. Qiú (Small dragon)

E. 奈   5. Nài (But)

#135.

A. 馍   1. Xī (Alkene)

B. 坊   2. Mó (Steamed bread)

C. 驾   3. Yù (A surname)

D. 尉   4. Jià (Harness)

E. 烯   5. Fáng (Workshop)

#136.

A. 讨   1. Hàn (Peng)

B. 孚   2. Gá (A traditional Chinese folk toy for children)

C. 翰   3. Yī (One)

D. 尜   4. Fú (Inspire confidence in sb)

E. 弌   5. Tǎo (Discuss)

#137.

A. 跑   1. Huò (Goods)

B. 板   2. Páo (Dig ground with foot or hoof)

C. 货   3. Tuó (A small bay in a river)

D. 柜   4. Guì (Cupboard)

E. 沱   5. Bǎn (Board)

#138.

A. 棕   1. Tuì (Scald in order to remove hairs or feathers)

B. 魅   2. Cǎi (Variegated color)

C. 彩   3. Nèi (Inside)

D. 煺   4. Zōng (Brown)

E. 内   5. Mèi (Goblin)

#139.

A. 觑   1. Shāo (A little)

B. 稍   2. Hú (Falcon)

C. 耶   3. Yē (Jesus)

D. 灿   4. Càn (Bright)

E. 鹘   5. Qù (Look)

#140.

A. 汶   1. Chèn (Take advantage of)

B. 炸   2. Wèn (Short for the Wenshui River)

C. 擎   3. Qíng (Prop up)

D. 累   4. Léi (Tie)

E. 趁   5. Zhá (Fry in deep fat or oil)

#141.

A. 郰   1. Juǎn (Embroil)

B. 捶   2. Shì (Room)

C. 龌   3. Wò (Dirty)

D. 室   4. Chuí (Hammer)

E. 卷   5. Yún (A surname)

#142.

A. 质   1. Qīng (Blue or green)

B. 妻   2. Jǐng (Trap)

C. 斤   3. Zhì (Nature)

D. 青   4. Jīn (Jin, a unit of weight (0.5Kg))

E. 阱   5. Qì (Marry a girl to (a man))

#143.

A. 杞   1. Sù (Sincere feeling)

B. 愫   2. Lá (Slash)

C. 拉   3. Shǒu (Stem)

D. 龈   4. Qǐ (Qi, a state in the Zhou Dynasty)

E. 艏   5. Yín (Gum)

#144.

A. 灯   1. Ráng (Pulp)

B. 他   2. Pī (Pi (an ancient place in Jiangsu Province))

C. 了   3. Liào (To survey)

D. 邳   4. Dēng (Lamp)

E. 瓤　　　　　　　　5. Tā (He)

#145.

A. 采　　　　　　　　1. Cài (Feudal estate)

B. 阴　　　　　　　　2. Jiè (Fall due)

C. 怜　　　　　　　　3. Yīn (Yin, the feminine or negative principle in nature)

D. 釉　　　　　　　　4. Yòu (Glaze (of porcelain))

E. 届　　　　　　　　5. Lián (Feel tender toward)

#146.

A. 匐　　　　　　　　1. Jǔ (Collect)

B. 隙　　　　　　　　2. Xì (Crack)

C. 辟　　　　　　　　3. Kào (Lean against)

D. 靠　　　　　　　　4. Fú (Creep)

E. 弆　　　　　　　　5. Pì (Open up)

#147.

A. 鉴　　　　　　　　1. Xiū (Embellish)

B. 修　　　　　　　　2. Fù (Repeated)

C. 复　　　　　　　　3. Jiàn (Ancient bronze mirror)

D. 摹　　　　　　　　4. Zhòu (Daytime)

E. 昼   5. Mó (Trace)

#148.

A. 崇   1. Sì (Wanton)

B. 肆   2. Dié (Septuagenarian)

C. 龅   3. Bāo (Bucktooth)

D. 禁   4. Chóng (High)

E. 耋   5. Jìn (Prohibit)

#149.

A. 弼   1. Bì (Assist)

B. 辜   2. Xiōng (Chest)

C. 匈   3. Gū (Crime)

D. 衲   4. Yàn (Elegant)

E. 彦   5. Nà (Patch up)

#150.

A. 正   1. Zhèng (Positive)

B. 乩   2. Lǚ (Repeatedly)

C. 宛   3. Qié (A surname)

D. 屡   4. Wǎn (As if)

E. 泥   5. Nì (Cover or daub with plaster, putty, etc.)

ANSWERS (1-150)

#1.	C. Hái		B. Zhì	E. Jiǎo	A. Fú	D. Qiū
A. Biāo	D. Diān	#44.	C. Bó		B. Máng	E. Fàn
B. Chuàn	E. Duàn	A. Zhī	D. Tū	#87.	C. Qī	
C. Fèi		B. Fàn	E. Zhào	A. Mó	D. Biāo	#130.
D. Chī	#23.	C. Lì		B. Gǒng	E. Shǎo	A. Luō
E. Dān	A. Gào	D. Kǎo	#66.	C. Bāng		B. Jùn
	B. Zhì	E. Fù	A. Chuàn	D. Fén	#109.	C. Qiū
#2.	C. Zhēn		B. Lián	E. Rùn	A. Liáng	D. Jīn
A. Lì	D. Guān	#45.	C. Gē		B. Yào	E. Biāo
B. Pèi	E. Wù	A. Xiá	D. Zhào	#88.	C. Bèi	
C. Shuì		B. Pàng	E. Yàn	A. Xún	D. Jié	#131.
D. Nì	#24.	C. Zōng		B. Lǐ	E. Páo	A. Zhān
E. Jiān	A. Chuāng	D. Cuān	#67.	C. Nüè		B. Jiù
	B. Kuí	E. Huá	A. Tǎn	D. Chǐ	#110.	C. Jǔ
#3.	C. Yā		B. Mèi	E. Yǐ	A. Shì	D. Yù
A. Zhū	D. Xīng	#46.	C. Kuò		B. Yùn	E. Shèn
B. Qiǎo	E. Guī	A. Dān	D. Yā	#89.	C. Jù	
C. Nǐng		B. Gěn	E. Bīn	A. Piáo	D. Jǐng	#132.
D. Dié	#25.	C. Bù		B. Zòng	E. Xuàn	A. Ǎo
E. Tì	A. Mù	D. Lún	#68.	C. Biàn		B. Yì
	B. Pō	E. Yù	A. Nǐng	D. Xiàng	#111.	C. Lú
#4.	C. Cuō		B. Yù	E. Lèng	A. Bù	D. Yù
A. Lǎo	D. Nà	#47.	C. Guì		B. Yì	E. Jiàng
B. Jiào	E. Ruò	A. Pò	D. Liú	#90.	C. Lěng	
C. Lì		B. Míng	E. Xiàng	A. Dòu	D. Fèn	#133.
D. Sì	#26.	C. Jiào		B. Jià	E. Diāo	A. Pèi
E. Kù	A. Péi	D. Cuān	#69.	C. Wèi		B. Niè
	B. Jiàn	E. Liè	A. Ēi	D. Nǎo	#112.	C. Zhǐ
#5.	C. Qì		B. Juàn	E. Kuǎn	A. Zhī	D. Zhào
A. Chōng	D. Xiào	#48.	C. Gān		B. Tā	E. Huī
B. Mǐn	E. Xuàn	A. Biǎn	D. Yǎn	#91.	C. Rú	
C. Hún		B. Jì	E. Zhài	A. Bāo	D. Zú	#134.
D. Piāo	#27.	C. Guāng		B. Hù	E. Yán	A. Níng
E. Lù	A. Dōng	D. Cù	#70.	C. Yuán		B. Qiú

	B. Qiān	E. Lín	A. Huáng	D. Àn	#113.	C. Qū
#6.	C. Gāo		B. Lóng	E. Jué	A. Guī	D. Nòng
A. Shì	D. Jìng	#49.	C. Kěn		B. Duì	E. Nài
B. Bó	E. Sì	A. Gāo	D. Qíng	#92.	C. Xiàng	
C. Shāo		B. Xiè	E. Fěi	A. Lún	D. Páo	#135.
D. Qià	#28.	C. Míng		B. Jù	E. Shǒu	A. Mó
E. Dí	A. Chào	D. Zhé	#71.	C. Éi		B. Fáng
	B. Pàng	E. Qiān	A. Mù	D. Shuì	#114.	C. Jià
#7.	C. Fǔ		B. Fán	E. Chóu	A. Pāi	D. Yù
A. Tā	D. Dàn	#50.	C. Hàn		B. Wàng	E. Xī
B. Jí	E. Zǎo	A. Qī	D. Nòng	#93.	C. Yù	
C. Jiàng		B. Xī	E. Pǐ	A. Féng	D. Ná	#136.
D. Liáng	#29.	C. Zhā		B. Mò	E. Shā	A. Tǎo
E. Wā	A. Fēng	D. Chào	#72.	C. Gòng		B. Fú
	B. Páng	E. Liáng	A. Dǎo	D. Tiǎo	#115.	C. Hàn
#8.	C. Chì		B. Tí	E. Gǎn	A. Gōng	D. Gá
A. Wài	D. Mín	#51.	C. Zhī		B. Ruò	E. Yī
B. Wèi	E. Mán	A. Ào	D. Shǐ	#94.	C. Bèi	
C. Tǎn		B. Xū	E. Jiān	A. Gòu	D. Xún	#137.
D. Shòu	#30.	C. Xiàng		B. Sǎn	E. Zuò	A. Páo
E. Shà	A. Dá	D. Cūn	#73.	C. Zhào		B. Bǎn
	B. Nüè	E. Hū	A. Jiān	D. Jiāo	#116.	C. Huò
#9.	C. Liàng		B. Jiǎ	E. Hú	A. Tǔn	D. Guì
A. Fěi	D. Hōng	#52.	C. Bān		B. Liáo	E. Tuó
B. Bān	E. Bì	A. Huì	D. Mǎi	#95.	C. Jū	
C. Zhǎn		B. Zhōng	E. Bā	A. Bān	D. Shèng	#138.
D. Qiè	#31.	C. Lù		B. Dì	E. Wán	A. Zōng
E. Ān	A. Zài	D. Nú	#74.	C. Miù		B. Mèi
	B. Huī	E. Sù	A. Liǎn	D. È	#117.	C. Cǎi
#10.	C. Jīn		B. Dài	E. Jiào	A. Yíng	D. Tuì
A. Kuàng	D. Tóng	#53.	C. Lǚ		B. Biě	E. Nèi
B. Gē	E. Zhōu	A. Tán	D. Qù	#96.	C. Shǔ	
C. Wán		B. Jié	E. Zhàng	A. Huó	D. Lù	#139.
D. Yào	#32.	C. Kě		B. Liáng	E. Fáng	A. Qù
E. Zhū	A. Bǔ	D. Bān	#75.	C. Jiè		B. Shāo
	B. Fàn	E. Náo	A. Áo	D. Yǐ	#118.	C. Yē

#11.	C. Yuān		B. Lín	E. Zōng	A. Jiàn	D. Càn
A. Yī	D. Lián	#54.	C. Xīng		B. Yú	E. Hú
B. Yì	E. Zhǐ	A. Qiāo	D. Qī	#97.	C. Fèi	
C. Bà		B. Qǐ	E. Pà	A. Ōu	D. Jiǎo	#140.
D. Sōu	#33.	C. Cuò		B. Tún	E. Dǎ	A. Wèn
E. Yàng	A. Zhǔ	D. Chèn	#76.	C. Qǐng		B. Zhá
	B. Jìn	E. Jù	A. Tàng	D. Le	#119.	C. Qíng
#12.	C. Qiǎo		B. Sǒng	E. Xuě	A. Jiā	D. Léi
A. Kū	D. Wù	#55.	C. Shǔ		B. Mǐn	E. Chèn
B. Dì	E. Mì	A. Kuàng	D. Tiǎo	#98.	C. Táo	
C. Qīng		B. Xūn	E. Hóng	A. Yǔ	D. Zhì	#141.
D. Tuì	#34.	C. È		B. Ěr	E. Lóng	A. Yún
E. Wēng	A. Lín	D. Ài	#77.	C. Biàn		B. Chuí
	B. Dá	E. Gòu	A. Jú	D. Qǐ	#120.	C. Wò
#13.	C. Jiāo		B. Pǎng	E. Xī	A. Lóu	D. Shì
A. Tí	D. Zhuǎn	#56.	C. Mì		B. Hù	E. Juǎn
B. Qìng	E. Shāo	A. Lǐ	D. Què	#99.	C. Tí	
C. Qián		B. Zhuì	E. Quán	A. Láng	D. Zhì	#142.
D. Luó	#35.	C. Mì		B. Yī	E. Wū	A. Zhì
E. Lǐn	A. Dú	D. Zhāo	#78.	C. Kuǎn		B. Qì
	B. Pò	E. Yǒng	A. Tàn	D. Zhì	#121.	C. Jīn
#14.	C. Háo		B. Zhāo	E. Jù	A. Sū	D. Qīng
A. Zhuó	D. Láng	#57.	C. Tú		B. Wèi	E. Jǐng
B. Zhé	E. Zhǐ	A. Ruǎn	D. Shāng	#100.	C. Pēng	
C. Shì		B. Liàn	E. Zhuàng	A. Sù	D. Táng	#143.
D. Gāng	#36.	C. Qià		B. Chú	E. Zōu	A. Qǐ
E. Liè	A. Liǎn	D. Chūn	#79.	C. Jià		B. Sù
	B. Yáo	E. Pì	A. Liào	D. Yūn	#122.	C. Lá
#15.	C. Táng		B. Zuò	E. Quǎn	A. Xī	D. Yín
A. Qí	D. Qiǎo	#58.	C. Shū		B. Jué	E. Shǒu
B. É	E. Zhǐ	A. Zhān	D. Lì	#101.	C. Bēi	
C. Pǐ		B. Shì	E. Lǜ	A. Qiào	D. Guǎn	#144.
D. Cān	#37.	C. Zé		B. Fāng	E. Páo	A. Dēng
E. Pī	A. Xiáng	D. Bì	#80.	C. Yì		B. Tā
	B. Shāng	E. Níng	A. Fù	D. Yíng	#123.	C. Liào
#16.	C. Dàng		B. Dài	E. É	A. Hésè	D. Pī

A. Suí	D. Zhǔ	#59.	C. Chù		B. Wū	E. Ráng
B. Tíng	E. Hǎo	A. Lóng	D. Cháng	#102.	C. Cī	
C. Mǎi		B. Juān	E. Yáo	A. Chǐ	D. Bāo	#145.
D. Yīng	#38.	C. Róng		B. Nú	E. Jiǔ	A. Cài
E. Tāng	A. Guān	D. Sòng	#81.	C. Kuàng		B. Yīn
	B. Tián	E. Pǎng	A. Jiù	D. Cōng	#124.	C. Lián
#17.	C. Fū		B. Niàn	E. Diàn	A. Qīng	D. Yòu
A. Hún	D. Xiòng	#60.	C. Bèi		B. Mò	E. Jiè
B. Yán	E. Dèng	A. Tīng	D. Lèi	#103.	C. Yī	
C. Huán		B. Dìng	E. Bèi	A. Fá	D. Zhuō	#146.
D. Chì	#39.	C. Suí		B. Fèi	E. Bǔ	A. Fú
E. Kuí	A. Sī	D. Chūn	#82.	C. Jié		B. Xì
	B. Yè	E. Biàn	A. Wéi	D. Gá	#125.	C. Pì
#18.	C. Xiāo		B. Qiān	E. Xiǎng	A. Kuí	D. Kào
A. Fēng	D. Hú	#61.	C. Qiú		B. Jiàng	E. Jǔ
B. Jǐn	E. Lián	A. Tán	D. Yì	#104.	C. Jì	
C. Jiē		B. Měng	E. Tuì	A. Luán	D. Xiàn	#147.
D. Hóu	#40.	C. Jué		B. Mín	E. Chǎo	A. Jiàn
E. Yǔ	A. Fù	D. Guān	#83.	C. Miè		B. Xiū
	B. Ōu	E. Qiǎn	A. Nài	D. Chào	#126.	C. Fù
#19.	C. Zhuàn		B. Chóng	E. Zōu	A. Ní	D. Mó
A. Tùn	D. Shā	#62.	C. Dì		B. Dāng	E. Zhòu
B. Pàn	E. Yǒu	A. Bàn	D. Sū	#105.	C. Qǐ	
C. Suǒ		B. Lòu	E. Jú	A. Gěng	D. Guǎ	#148.
D. Lì	#41.	C. Qián		B. Mǎn	E. Shè	A. Chóng
E. Qiān	A. É	D. Suàn	#84.	C. Hóng		B. Sì
	B. Jué	E. Xiàn	A. Xí	D. Fáng	#127.	C. Bāo
#20.	C. Kān		B. Yuàn	E. Tí	A. Yīng	D. Jìn
A. Guǐ	D. Lù	#63.	C. Suí		B. Lóu	E. Dié
B. Liú	E. Rán	A. Bì	D. Wéi	#106.	C. Xún	
C. Guài		B. Zhà	E. Nóng	A. Náo	D. Kě	#149.
D. Sān	#42.	C. Pán		B. Ěr	E. Shà	A. Bì
E. Fú	A. Sù	D. Zhǔ	#85.	C. Dān		B. Gū
	B. Zǎo	E. Ǎi	A. Lè	D. Méi	#128.	C. Xiōng
#21.	C. Zhé		B. Yǎn	E. Gěn	A. Lì	D. Nà
A. Zhēn	D. Kuài	#64.	C. Zēng		B. Mài	E. Yàn

B. Dīng	E. Qiān	A. Dǐ	D. Hù	#107.	C. gèn	
C. Lào		B. Guǐ	E. Jì	A. Yuè	D. Huì	#150.
D. Yāng	#43.	C. Huī		B. Huàn	E. Shā	A. Zhèng
E. Hú	A. Yāo	D. Háo	#86.	C. Bì		B. Qié
	B. Dí	E. Huài	A. Bàng	D. Gǒng	#129.	C. Wǎn
#22.	C. Qiān		B. Bó	E. Jué	A. Gǔ	D. Lǚ
A. Yù	D. Lín	#65.	C. Shān		B. Lǜ	E. Nì
B. Bì	E. Bà	A. Lì	D. Ruǎn	#108.	C. Mián	

Milton Keynes UK
Ingram Content Group UK Ltd.
UKHW051030221123
433051UK00018B/701